Glendale Library, Arts & Culture Dept.

3 9 0 1 0 0 5 6 8 4 0 9 8 0

D0884694

NO LONGER PROPERTY OF
GLENDALE PUBLIC LIBRARY

TOOLS FOR TEACHERS

- **ATOS:** 0.5
- **GRL:** C
- **WORD COUNT:** 33

- **CURRICULUM CONNECTIONS:** community, recreation

Skills to Teach

- **HIGH-FREQUENCY WORDS:** a, fun, go, have, in, on, our, play, the, to, with
- **CONTENT WORDS:** dog, grass, lie, park, picnic, playground, swings
- **PUNCTUATION:** periods, apostrophe, exclamation point
- **WORD STUDY:** compound word (*playground*); r-controlled vowel (*park*); /ng/ (*swing, swings*); dipthong /ou/ (*playground*)
- **TEXT TYPE:** information report

Before Reading Activities

- Read the title and give a simple statement of the main idea.
- Have students "walk" though the book and talk about what they see in the pictures.
- Introduce new vocabulary by having students predict the first letter and locate the word in the text.
- Discuss any unfamiliar concepts that are in the text.

After Reading Activities

Encourage children to talk about their experiences at a park. What do they like to do there? What kinds of things do they see? Discuss their answers as a group.

Tadpole Books are published by Jump!, 5357 Penn Avenue South, Minneapolis, MN 55419, www.jumplibrary.com

Copyright ©2018 Jump! International copyright reserved in all countries. No part of this book may be reproduced in any form without written permission from the publisher.

Editorial: Hundred Acre Words, LLC **Designer:** Anna Peterson

Photo Credits: Alamy: Blue Jean Images, 6–7. iStock: FatCamera, 2–3, 10–11; fstop123, 4–5; NI QIN, 4–5; pioneer111, cover. Shutterstock: alexsaz, 4–5; pernasanitfoto, cover; Sergey Novikov, 12–13, 14–15; Sergiy Kuzmin, 1; Trong Nguyen, 16; unguryanu, 8–9.

Library of Congress Cataloging-in-Publication Data
Names: Donner, Erica, author.
Title: Park / by Erica Donner.
Description: Minneapolis, Minnesota: Jump!, Inc., 2017. | Series: Around town | Includes index. | Audience: Ages 3 to 6.
Identifiers: LCCN 2017033833 (print) | LCCN 2017024208 (ebook) | ISBN 9781624967139 (ebook) | ISBN 9781620319291 (hardcover: alk. paper) | ISBN 9781620319307 (pbk.)
Subjects: LCSH: Play—Juvenile literature. | Urban parks—Juvenile literature.
Classification: LCC GV182.9 (print) | LCC GV182.9 .D66 2017 (ebook) | DDC 790—dc23
LC record available at https://lccn.loc.gov/2017033833

PARK

by Erica Donner

TABLE OF CONTENTS

Park 2

Words to Know 16

Index 16

j 790 DON

PARK

Let's go to the park.

We play on the playground.

We have a picnic.

dog

We play with our dog.

We lie in the grass.

We swing on
the swings.

We have fun!

WORDS TO KNOW

dog

grass

park

picnic

playground

swings

INDEX

dog 9

fun 15

grass 11

park 3

picnic 7

play 5, 9

playground 5

swings 13